Owl Spirit

POEMS AFFIRMATIONS
SCRIBES & STORYTELLING

Owl Spirit

POEMS AFFIRMATIONS
SCRIBES & STORYTELLING

COPYRIGHT © 2022 ARAYA S. KNIGHT

ALL RIGHTS RESERVED.

ISBN: 978-0-578-38442-9
ISBN-13: 978-0-578-38442-9

DEDICATION

Thank you God for trusting me with your people. I know this because you are the source of the power and gifts that I possess

Thank you ancestors, I am you and you are me. Thank you guides, spirit animals, mother nature

Thank you, me, for always choosing me

To my eldest son, Ahmeer, Thank you for growing with me. Always Remember what I told you.

My son, Nasir aka twin, you heal the world every time you smile.

My son, Adonis, protect your heart and keep it open.

As Life Does flow

OWL SPIRIT

ACKNOWLEDGMENTS

Thank you, Ms. Inya, Victoria salter, Sensay9, Shay, Uncuttart, Vinx De'jon Parette, Tommy Jackson, Tasha Russell, , Miles s., Edgar s. Diaz, for inspiration, for your encouragement, for your assistance , divine moments, and your time. it's been a long journey. I love you all.

DECEMBER 28,2021, 17:51

HEART CHAKRA

Wondering through a tropical rain forest,
With every imprint these footsteps make,
Source flows through my sole,
Waterfalls expectedly springing through unexpected territories.
As my albino serpent smooths my waist,
Nature's beauty surrounds me.
Yet still my soul longs.
Owl Spirit,
Will I ever find you?
My heart is open now...
Your words lie engraved in my heart.
Return to me,
As you spoke.

A MOMENT IN MIAMI

The calm,
The reminder,
Stop and smell the flowers,
So intertwined in meaningless distractions,
That I may have missed an opportunity,
A golden ticket,
Watching me from afar,
Admiring my fire within,
But knowing I'm not quite there yet,
Hurting my seer's soul,

Sitting at the bar,
He then whispered, "Just let it go"
Oh, but my Anger felt otherwise,

And my inner soul cried,
"I can't let that shit go!"

The pale man shook his head and smiled.
For he already planted his seed.

He spread his towel pool side,
Put on his shades,
Relaxed,
Laid back,
And continued to watch me grow.

WISDOM

Oh, my Sister,
My nearest Kin,
Who protects me from the immoral,
I will always keep you close.
My bosom is where your head lay.
Iniabasi.
There lies Agape.
Gentler than a Mother's touch,
Yet stronger than my Father's foundation,
More intimate than my Lover's caress,
Steadier than a child's affection.

THE ELEPHANT IN THE ROOM

    I cannot change the past,
    But I can make my future,
    Every single moment of my life,
    Was meant to happen the way it happened.
    I am Light.
    I am Truth.
    I walk in Truth.
    I acknowledge and accept what IS.
    No matter mine or others' perception,
    Only the DEEPEST Truth Do I Accept.
    Ase.

BREAK THE CHAIN

In order to break ancestral karma there were some things I had to do in order to feel that it was wrong so that I could set those after me, free.

A Moment

I had a breakthrough with my Mother.
We had a moment.
A turning effect,
Produced by a force,
Acting at a distance,
On an object.
I had a moment with my Father.
Me and my Brother had a moment too.
An appropriate time for doing something,
An opportunity.
My Sister had a moment with me,
My Sister.
A particular stage in someone's development,
Or rather in a course of events.
I've had moments with my Children,
Importance.
Friends,
A brief moment in time.
I've had moments with Myself,
A point in time,
Necessary,
I deserve it.
Pain, Joy, Anxiety, Frustration, Anger...
I embrace you,
The window to my soul,
I love YOU.

AFFIRMATION

I am so confident in my purpose that I am so confident my passion will produce my income.

JANUARY 12, 2022, 19:01

COMPLETE

I cry so that I can smile,
As a thorn is to a rose.
I have loved with all my being,
Those that have entered my home,
Have robbed me of precious gems.
So,
I hope that you can understand,
Why I protect my heart.
Abandonment.
Every person in my life,
At some point,
So when my desires are fulfilled,
The fear of losing it makes me question,
Will you leave me too?
So I won't compel you to stay.
Cry now.
So I can continue to smile.
And cling to the knowing,
That I am complete,
No matter.
Ase..

JANUARY 18, 2022, FINISHED 10:55

I am The Gift.
Every day, Ase.

JANUARY 18, 2022, FINISHED 11:01AM

Observing without judgement and being kind to myself and others, Gravitate to me, those that have light energy, whose hearts' are pure, Ase.

BALANCE

I am free,
I embrace my desires.
I acknowledge them.
I am aware that emotions are deep.
I allow myself to feel them,
But they do not control me.

JANUARY 8, 2022, 19:04

Distance those that bring harm to me by blessing me with discernment.

Being hurt by someone that does not understand the pain they cause me, let alone what they are doing, is far more dangerous than being harmed by someone that knows exactly what they are doing and the harm they bring to me.

Tank on E

I was told this journey would be long.
Extended so,
That it would cause my subconscious to grow forgetful.
I had been walking in my gifts all along.
Drifting in spirit,
Allowing the Mirage to sift of my energy.
Not a gas station in miles.
I knew what I signed up for.
Many of my ancestors have attempted but did not succeed.
The real time of this journey far outweighed the description.
Giving to the weak,
Now running on fumes.
Visioned blurred yet still steadfast.
My steps lead me to an oasis.
I am filled-poured in to.
No longer depleted,
I am renewed.
I am surrounded by mirrors,
You reflect me.
If I see it in you,
I can see it in me.

I am I am.   I am I a
I am I am. I.   I am I am I
I am I am I am I am I am I I
am not strong, I am divine. I am
not weak, I'm vulnerable. I am
not powerless, I am power full.

Know the difference.

Respectfully,
Ase.

January 14, 2022, Finished 20:02

I Innerstand

Oh lover,
Oh lover,
Who brought me much grief,
Your greatest mistake,
Was to leave me with me.
When I am with me,
As my tears soak the tree.
My young seeds mature.
I rise from the floor.
As clouds transform,
As do I,
They pour.
Now I may wallow in my pool,
But my roots,
Deep. In.
I may start from below,
But home is where my heart is.
I remember My Worth.
I know what was spoken.
I cannot sore if I cage myself within.

This Dance

My soul has been having a slow burning dance with God.
Slow deep breathes,
Naturally in the moment,
But suddenly I picture myself in a state of frustration,
Sulking,
And God,
With a slight touch,
Pushes my chin towards him,
Attempting to grasp my attention.
And we're in this tender dance,
But my eyes are flustered by the crowd,
And every time he touches my face,
He espies my eyes.
With every descry
There lies a moment of Euphoria.
I am Safe.
I gasped the depth of him.
And in this moment,
I AM.
And in the richness of time,
I become vertigo.
Discombobulated,
From trying to keep pace with the crowd.
He graces my chin once more,
And I surrender into his gaze.
I am at the helm of him.
My eye opens completely.
And I AM.
Flowing in the Know.
And every day I AM.

I gave in to the dance.
Every day is Euphoria.
I am no other than me.
And many gifts are in me.
My flaws are flawless.
They are now the footprints in this dance.

February 5, 2022, finished 19:17

Death to Ego

Truth comes from my heart. Ego comes from anything outside of it. I will not concern myself in the matters of those who receive truth through the lens of ego. Speak from my heart or do not speak at all. How truth is received is no business of mine. I am aligned with universe.

Word From the Wise

When it's to the point that I can avoid it; That's when it becomes a choice.

Sometimes I feel I don't have control, but it is because it has become a habit.

I am aware.

I know what I have to do.

I just have to do it.

When I am truly tired of the cycle I completely avoid anything that takes me down the same path.

I find another route completely and other paths begin to open.

January 5, 2022, 7:25

Be myself. I AM Sexy. I AM beautiful. I AM divine. I AM compassionate. I AM a person with integrity. My heart is open. I AM protected. I AM the gift. I speak truth. I AM light. I AM the Creator. I AM complete. I Know what I like. I Know what I want. I water myself before I water others. Home is everywhere I AM because I'm unshakably

me!

December 29, 2021, 19:01

Free 99

Succumb to my desires,
But know I am complete,
Though earth manipulates,
I am still as is a tree.
Emotions touch deep.
Like the sea,
So is the sky.
Judged.
Enslaved.
I swim.
I fly.
What am I?

January 26, 2022 20:45

If Spiders Could Talk

Please don't fear me,
I'm only a Projection of who you should be,
Independent,
I move freely,
Everything I need is within me.
Truly I see,
That I scare me,
It has nothing to do with you,
I fear the power in me.
So next time you see me trapped,
Free me if you can,
I must have lost my way after leaving my spiderman.
No worries,
I will always find my way.
Home is me.
I'll find my clan.
Look at me,
And you'll see your reflection.

January 26, 2022 18:08

Better Out Than In

Speak your truth,
Or the outside will.
If you say nothing,
The outside won't yield.
Your silence still speaks,
What your mouth won't appeal.
So be careful that your tongue,
Leads the front of your heel.

Finished 18:33

January 25, 2022 2:00

One day, while driving, I felt an urge to go near the water. I went for a drive and parked. As I sat parked near the river I watched as the birds few overhead. As I looked out to the river, a Raven landed on the sign right in front of me. The Raven turned their body towards me and crowded 7 times, They then flew to a nearby light pole and there sat another Raven. They for but a moment sat next to one another. Then, they flew in two directions towards the sky. As they flew apart, so did they meet again, in the tree. Their home, where they lay.

Finished at 2:15

February 2, 2022, 15:44

Earth Angel

I don't come here often,
But when One calls me,
I come.
Now I will admit,
The assignment at first glance was uninviting,
But I was told to keep reading,
And so I did,
And the more I read,
I seen a long journey ahead.
The reward is as wide as my eyes can see,
And as much as my heart can desire.
Yes, that sounds nice.
Oh, but wisdom is priceless.
Hidden in plain sight,
Observing you all and living the human experience.
So, that I could dig up the gems that needed to be found.
For if I reveal my identity,
You would not commit your crime.
My sacrifices are for the greater good of mankind.
And I am here to serve the One who flows through all.

Finished 16:06

ABOUT THE AUTHOR

Araya Knight is originally native to North Carolina. Born into a military family, she has traveled throughout the states but eventually settling in Florida with her three children.

9 780578 384429

www.ingramcontent.com/pod-product-compliance
Lightning Source LLC
Chambersburg PA
CBHW051544230426
43669CB00015B/2719